Lorraine Kelly

In the lush, vibrant landscapes of Scotland, under the watchful gaze of ancient castles and amidst the whispers of history, Lorraine Smith was born on a chilly autumn day, November 30th, 1959. Her voice, destined to echo through the hearts and homes of many, began its journey in the quietude of Scottish life, nurtured by the rich tapestry of culture and tradition that surrounded her. Lorraine, a name now synonymous with warmth, charisma, and a pioneering spirit in British television, embarked on a path that would lead her to become an emblem of resilience and versatility in the world of media.

Her career, a mosaic of diverse roles and achievements, commenced in the theatrical realm, where Lorraine's passion for storytelling and her innate ability to connect with an audience first shone. This foundation in the arts, coupled with her natural eloquence and curiosity, paved the way for a seamless transition into television. Lorraine's journey through the British broadcasting landscape began with ITV and STV, where her authenticity and warmth in front of the camera quickly endeared her to the nation.

As the host of "Good Morning Britain" from 1988 to 1992, Lorraine's morning greetings became a staple in homes across the UK, her voice a comforting presence that accompanied the sunrise. Her tenure on "GMTV" from 1993 to 2010 further solidified her status as a beloved figure in British television, a constant through the ever-changing tides of news and entertainment. Lorraine's versatility shone through her work on "This Morning" and "Daybreak," where she brought stories to life, shared in the nation's joys and sorrows, and became a trusted face of daytime TV.

However, it was not just in the realm of morning and daytime television that Lorraine made her mark. Her eponymous programme "Lorraine," which began in 2010 and continues to this day, showcases her unique ability to blend journalism, entertainment, and heartfelt conversations, creating a space where viewers feel both informed and uplifted. Beyond the studio, Lorraine's dedication to public service and philanthropy found a powerful outlet in her roles with the "STV Children's Appeal" and "The Sun Military Awards," reflecting her deep commitment to giving back to the community and supporting those in need.

Lorraine's contributions to broadcasting, journalism, and charity have not gone unnoticed. Her appointment as Officer of the Order of the British Empire (OBE) in the 2012 New Year Honours was a testament to her impact off-screen, particularly her tireless charity work. This recognition was further elevated in 2020 when she was promoted to Commander of the Order of the British Empire (CBE) for her services to broadcasting, journalism, and charity, a rare and distinguished honor that speaks volumes of her professional excellence and personal integrity.

Perhaps one of the most distinctive chapters in Lorraine's illustrious career was her tenure as Rector of the University of Dundee from 2004 to 2007, a role that underscored her commitment to education and her ability to inspire the next generation. In this capacity, she was not just a figurehead but a mentor, a leader, and an advocate for student empowerment, leaving an indelible mark on the academic community.

Lorraine Smith's story is not just one of personal achievement but of how genuine warmth, relentless dedication, and a passion for making a difference can illuminate the lives of millions. From the stages of Scotland to the screens of the nation, her journey continues to be an inspiring saga of grace, resilience, and the power of communication. In a world often divided, Lorraine stands as a beacon of unity, reminding us of the shared stories that connect us all.

Despite the spotlight and accolades, Lorraine remains grounded in her roots, drawing strength from her Scottish heritage and the values instilled in her from a young age. Born into a family where hard work and kindness were cherished above all else, she carries these principles with her, infusing every aspect of her career with authenticity and empathy.

Away from the cameras, Lorraine's life is a testament to balance and resilience. Amidst the whirlwind of television schedules and public appearances, she finds solace in her passions outside of work. A talented singer, her melodic voice echoes through the corridors of her home, a reminder of the joy found in creativity and self-expression. Whether performing on stage or simply singing to herself, music remains a constant source of inspiration and rejuvenation.

Family, too, occupies a central place in Lorraine's heart. As a devoted wife and mother, she cherishes the quiet moments spent with loved ones, finding fulfillment in the simple pleasures of shared laughter and conversation. Despite her demanding schedule, she prioritizes those closest to her, understanding that true success lies not in accolades or fame but in the bonds forged with those we hold dear.

As the years pass and her legacy continues to evolve, Lorraine remains steadfast in her commitment to making a difference. Through her platform and influence, she amplifies voices that might otherwise go unheard, championing causes close to her heart with unwavering dedication. Whether advocating for children's rights, supporting veterans, or raising awareness for charitable initiatives, she embodies the principle that true greatness is measured not by what we accomplish for ourselves, but by how we uplift others.

In the tapestry of British television, Lorraine Smith's story stands as a testament to the power of authenticity, resilience, and compassion. From her humble beginnings in Scotland to her status as a national treasure, she remains a guiding light in an ever-changing industry, a beacon of hope and inspiration for generations to come. And as the sun sets on each day, casting its golden glow upon the horizon, Lorraine's voice echoes in the hearts of millions, a reminder that even in the darkest of times, there is always a reason to smile.

In the heart of Glasgow, amidst the bustling streets of the Gorbals, Lorraine Smith came into the world on November 30, 1959. From her earliest days, she was surrounded by the vibrant energy and rich culture of her Scottish heritage, her roots intertwined with the fabric of this storied city. Yet, her time in Glasgow was brief, as her family soon embarked on a new chapter, setting their sights on the quieter streets of East Kilbride when Lorraine was just two years old.

It was in the welcoming embrace of East Kilbride that Lorraine's formative years unfolded. Surrounded by the rolling hills and gentle whispers of the countryside, she found herself enchanted by the wonders of the world around her. At Claremont High School, she eagerly absorbed knowledge, her curiosity driving her to explore new horizons and embrace every opportunity that came her way.

As graduation approached, Lorraine stood at a crossroads, her future beckoning with infinite possibilities. Despite the allure of university and the promise of academic pursuits, she followed her heart down a different path. Turning down a place to study English and Russian, she set her sights on a different kind of education—one rooted in the tangible realities of everyday life.

Joining the East Kilbride News, her local newspaper, Lorraine embarked on a journey that would shape the course of her career. Immersed in the world of journalism, she discovered a passion for storytelling, her words weaving tapestries of truth and insight for her community to behold. It was here, amidst the ink-stained pages and bustling newsroom, that she honed her craft, her determination and tenacity setting her apart from the crowd.

In 1983, Lorraine's path took an unexpected turn as she ventured into the realm of broadcasting, joining BBC Scotland as a researcher. This marked the beginning of a new chapter, one filled with boundless potential and untold adventures. Her keen intellect and unwavering dedication quickly caught the attention of her colleagues, propelling her forward on a trajectory of success.

By 1984, Lorraine had found her place in front of the camera, making her debut as an on-screen reporter for TV-am, where she covered Scottish news with poise and professionalism. Her journey from the streets of Glasgow to the airwaves of national television was a testament to her resilience and determination, her Irish ancestry infusing her work with a sense of pride and heritage.

Though her path was far from conventional, Lorraine's decision to forge her own way proved to be a stroke of brilliance. With each step she took, she carved out a niche for herself in the competitive world of broadcasting, her journey marked by courage, passion, and an unwavering commitment to excellence. And as she looked ahead to the countless adventures that lay on the horizon, one thing was abundantly clear—Lorraine Smith was destined for greatness.

With a fierce determination and a passion for storytelling burning brightly within her, Lorraine Smith embarked on her broadcasting journey in 1984, joining TV-am as Scotland Correspondent. It was a role that would set the stage for her meteoric rise in the world of television journalism.

From the outset, Lorraine approached her work with a rare blend of empathy and professionalism, immersing herself in the stories that shaped the fabric of Scottish life. But it was her coverage of the tragic Pan Am Flight 103 disaster in Lockerbie, in July 1989, that catapulted her into the national spotlight. Her compassionate reporting and unwavering commitment to truth and integrity captured the hearts of viewers across the country, earning her widespread acclaim and recognition.

Buoyed by the success of her coverage, Lorraine's star continued to ascend. In the summer of 1989, she took the helm of TV-am's Summer Sunday program alongside chief reporter Geoff Meade, showcasing her versatility and adaptability as a presenter. Her natural charm and effortless charisma endeared her to audiences, establishing her as a rising star in the world of morning television.

As 1989 drew to a close, Lorraine's talents caught the attention of TV-am's main weekday program, where she provided cover for the regular presenters. It was a pivotal moment in her career, a stepping stone towards even greater opportunities on the horizon.

Then, on January 31, 1990, Lorraine's journey reached a significant milestone as she assumed the role of main presenter on "Good Morning Britain," alongside Mike Morris. With her trademark warmth and infectious enthusiasm, she brought a fresh energy to the morning airwaves, captivating viewers with her engaging interviews and insightful commentary.

For Lorraine, "Good Morning Britain" was more than just a television program—it was a platform to connect with audiences, to share stories that mattered, and to make a positive impact on the world. With each passing day, she endeavored to uphold the highest standards of journalism, driven by a deep sense of responsibility to inform, educate, and inspire.

As the 1990s dawned, Lorraine's star continued to rise, her indomitable spirit and unwavering dedication propelling her towards ever-greater heights of success. Yet, amidst the glitz and glamour of the television industry, she remained grounded in her values, her commitment to authenticity and integrity guiding her every step of the way. And as she looked towards the future, Lorraine knew that the best was yet to come.

As the new millennium dawned, Lorraine's star continued to rise, and her show underwent various rebrandings to reflect the evolving landscape of morning television. From "GMTV Today" to "LK Today" and eventually "GMTV with Lorraine," she remained a constant presence on the airwaves, her warmth and authenticity resonating with audiences of all ages.

Yet, amidst the highs of her career, Lorraine faced challenges of her own. In 2007, she found herself embroiled in controversy when she was prevented from appearing in an advertising campaign for Asda, a decision that sparked public scrutiny and speculation. Despite the setback, Lorraine remained resilient, her unwavering dedication to her craft guiding her through turbulent waters.

In July 2010, as GMTV made way for "Daybreak," Lorraine bid farewell to the show that had been her home for over a decade. But it was not the end of her journey. On that same day, a new chapter began as she launched her eponymous program, "Lorraine," a testament to her enduring legacy in morning television.

As she took her final bow on GMTV, Lorraine Smith's journey was far from over. With a new show and endless possibilities on the horizon, she stood ready to embrace the next chapter of her illustrious career, her passion for broadcasting burning brighter than ever before. And as she stepped into the unknown, one thing was abundantly clear—Lorraine was ready to conquer whatever challenges lay ahead.

Since the dawn of the new decade in 2010, Lorraine Smith's indomitable spirit and boundless energy have continued to shape the landscape of British television. With the conclusion of GMTV, ITV Breakfast ushered in a new era, with Lorraine at the forefront, launching her eponymous show alongside the revamped "Daybreak." With a fresh new look and a renewed sense of purpose, Lorraine endeavored to bring her signature warmth and charm to morning audiences once again.

In addition to her role as host of "Lorraine," Lorraine embarked on a myriad of other projects, showcasing her versatility and adaptability as a broadcaster. In 2011, she took on the role of presenter for the ITV series "Children's Hospital," offering viewers an intimate glimpse into the world of pediatric medicine. Her guest appearance on the BBC Two series "Never Mind the Buzzcocks" further highlighted her comedic prowess and undeniable charisma, endearing her to audiences of all ages.

Yet, it was her voice-over work on the CBeebies show "Raa Raa the Noisy Lion" that truly captured the hearts of young viewers, cementing her status as a beloved figure in children's entertainment.

In 2012, Lorraine's star continued to rise as she stepped into the role of presenter on "Daybreak," following in the footsteps of Christine Bleakley. Alongside co-host Aled Jones, she brought her trademark warmth and authenticity to the morning airwaves, captivating audiences with her engaging interviews and insightful commentary.

However, in February 2014, Lorraine made the decision to leave "Daybreak" behind and focus solely on her own show, "Lorraine," which she began hosting five days a week from April 28, 2014. Her dedication to her own program was unwavering, and her return marked a new chapter in her broadcasting journey.

Throughout the years, Lorraine has continued to diversify her portfolio, taking on a variety of projects that showcase her versatility and range as a presenter. From her role as a reporter on "Good Morning Britain" to her cameo appearances on popular television shows like "Birds of a Feather" and "Coronation Street," she has proven time and again that she is a force to be reckoned with in the world of entertainment.

Even in the face of unprecedented challenges, such as the COVID-19 pandemic, Lorraine remained steadfast in her commitment to her viewers, hosting her program from the "Good Morning Britain" studio with a more news-focused approach. Yet, as the world slowly began to recover, she returned to her own studio, bringing her trademark warmth and positivity back to the airwaves once more.

As Lorraine continues to inspire and uplift audiences across the nation, her legacy as one of Britain's most beloved television personalities remains firmly intact. With each new project and every heartfelt interview, she reminds us all of the power of kindness, compassion, and the unwavering belief that, even in the darkest of times, there is always hope.

Lorraine Smith's dedication to philanthropy and community service has been a cornerstone of her career, extending far beyond the confines of the television studio. Since 2005, she has played a pivotal role in hosting the prestigious Glenfiddich Spirit of Scotland Awards for STV, showcasing the remarkable achievements and contributions of individuals across various fields.

Her commitment to making a difference in the lives of others became even more evident with her involvement in STV's Children's Appeal, beginning in 2011. Year after year, Lorraine has lent her voice and her platform to raise awareness and funds for this vital cause, joining forces with weather presenter Sean Batty to host the annual appeal telethon. Through her tireless efforts, she has helped to provide support and assistance to countless children and families in need, embodying the spirit of compassion and generosity.

In addition to her work with the Children's Appeal, Lorraine has also spearheaded various initiatives and programs on STV, showcasing her versatility as a presenter and her unwavering commitment to shining a light on important issues. From hosting the heartwarming "STV Appeal Stories" to bringing audiences together with her 2016 show "Lorraine & Friends," she has continued to use her platform for good, inspiring others to join her in making a positive impact on the world.

In 2016, Lorraine welcomed viewers into the New Year with a special edition of "Lorraine Kelly's Hogmanay," filmed aboard HM Frigate Unicorn in Dundee. Against the backdrop of celebration and camaraderie, she ushered in the New Year with warmth and joy, spreading cheer to all who tuned in.

Beyond her hosting duties, Lorraine has made memorable appearances on various STV programs, including the talk shows "The Riverside Show" and "The Late Show with Ewen Cameron." Her presence on these platforms has allowed her to engage with audiences in a more intimate and personal manner, fostering meaningful connections and sparking important conversations.

In 2019, Lorraine added yet another feather to her cap with her role as the presenter of the gameshow "The Cash Machine," bringing her trademark charm and wit to the small screen once again.

Through her work with STV, Lorraine Smith has proven herself to be not only a talented presenter but also a compassionate advocate for those in need. Her dedication to philanthropy and community service serves as an inspiration to us all, reminding us of the profound impact that one person can have when they use their voice and their platform for good.

Lorraine Smith's television career is a rich tapestry woven with diverse roles and memorable appearances, showcasing her versatility and talent as a presenter and personality.

During the mid-1990s, Lorraine stepped into the world of magazine programming as the presenter of Carlton's "After 5," bringing her trademark warmth and charm to the small screen. Her natural charisma and engaging style endeared her to audiences, establishing her as a familiar face in the world of daytime television.

In 2001, Lorraine made a memorable guest appearance on Lily Savage's "Blankety Blank," showcasing her comedic chops and quick wit alongside the legendary drag queen. Her presence added a touch of sparkle to the iconic game show, leaving audiences entertained and wanting more.

But it was her role as the national spokeswoman for the United Kingdom during the Eurovision Song Contest in 2003 and 2004 that truly showcased Lorraine's versatility as a presenter. Taking on the responsibility of collating votes and representing her country on an international stage, she navigated the complexities of live television with grace and professionalism, earning praise for her impeccable performance.

Throughout her career, Lorraine has also made numerous guest appearances on popular comedy panel shows, including "Have I Got News for You," where she showcased her sharp wit and infectious laughter. Her presence added a touch of humor and levity to the proceedings, earning her a place in the hearts of audiences nationwide.

In addition to her television work, Lorraine has also ventured into the world of documentary programming, hosting a variety of thought-provoking series that tackle important issues facing society. From "Secrets Revealed – DNA Stories" to "Lorraine Kelly's Big Fat Challenge," she has used her platform to shed light on topics ranging from missing persons to health and wellness, inspiring viewers to take action and make a difference.

Lorraine's acting talents have also been showcased on the small screen, with appearances in popular Scottish sitcoms like "Still Game" and the soap opera "River City." Her versatility as a performer has earned her praise from critics and audiences alike, solidifying her status as one of Britain's most beloved television personalities.

In 2021, Lorraine continued to captivate audiences with her insightful interviews, including a memorable conversation with Gurdeep Pandher. And in 2024, she surprised viewers as a contestant on the fifth series of "The Masked Singer," showcasing her adventurous spirit and willingness to embrace new challenges.

Through her varied television roles and appearances, Lorraine Smith has left an indelible mark on the world of entertainment, captivating audiences with her warmth, wit, and unwavering professionalism. As she continues to delight viewers with her infectious energy and genuine passion for storytelling, one thing is certain—Lorraine's star will continue to shine bright for years to come.

In addition to her illustrious career in television, Lorraine Smith has also made her mark as a talented writer, sharing her insights and wisdom with readers across the nation through her weekly columns.

For readers of The Sun, Lorraine's column is a beacon of light, offering a blend of wit, humor, and heartfelt commentary on topics ranging from current events to personal anecdotes. Her unique perspective and engaging writing style have earned her a dedicated following, as readers eagerly await her latest musings each week.

In The Sunday Post, Lorraine's column takes on a more reflective tone, delving into deeper themes and offering readers a moment of quiet contemplation amidst the hustle and bustle of daily life. Whether sharing her thoughts on family, relationships, or the world around us, she has a gift for connecting with readers on a personal level, leaving a lasting impression with every word she writes.

But perhaps one of Lorraine's most meaningful roles as a writer is her position as the first Agony Aunt for the Royal Air Force's RAF News. In this capacity, she offers support, guidance, and a listening ear to members of the RAF community, addressing their concerns and providing a source of comfort in times of need. Her compassionate approach and genuine empathy make her a trusted confidante to those she serves, embodying the spirit of service and camaraderie that defines the RAF.

Through her writing, Lorraine Smith continues to touch the hearts and minds of readers across the country, offering insight, inspiration, and a touch of warmth to brighten their days. Whether on the pages of a newspaper or the screens of a television set, her words resonate with authenticity and sincerity, leaving a lasting impact on all who have the privilege of reading them.

Lorraine Smith's compassion extends far beyond the realm of entertainment, as evidenced by her extensive charity work and philanthropic endeavors. As a celebrity patron of Worldwide Cancer Research, she lends her voice and her platform to raise awareness and funds for groundbreaking cancer research, offering hope to countless individuals and families affected by this devastating disease.

In addition to her work with Worldwide Cancer Research, Lorraine is a passionate advocate for human rights, serving as a patron of the charity POhWER. Through her involvement with POhWER, she helps empower individuals to find their voice, access the support they need, and seek justice in the face of adversity. Her commitment to championing the rights of others reflects her deeply held belief in the importance of compassion and solidarity.

Lorraine's dedication to supporting those in need extends to organizations such as Help for Heroes, where she serves as a patron. By honoring the sacrifices of servicemen and women and providing vital assistance to veterans and their families, Help for Heroes embodies Lorraine's belief in the power of community and service.

As an Honorary Patron of The Courtyard, Herefordshire's Centre for the Arts, Lorraine continues to enrich the lives of others through her support of the arts. Her commitment to promoting creativity and cultural enrichment reflects her belief in the transformative power of the arts to inspire, educate, and uplift.

Lorraine's philanthropic efforts extend beyond the borders of her homeland, as evidenced by her participation in the BT Red Nose Desert Trek for Comic Relief in 2011. By trekking through the Kaisut Desert and raising over £1.3 million for Comic Relief, she exemplified her dedication to making a positive impact on a global scale.

Since its inception in 2011, Lorraine has been an ambassador and presenter for the STV Children's Appeal, using her platform to shine a light on the needs of vulnerable children and families across Scotland. Her unwavering commitment to improving the lives of children underscores her belief in the importance of compassion, empathy, and solidarity.

In 2011, Lorraine expanded her philanthropic reach by becoming an ambassador for the charity Sightsavers, furthering her commitment to combating preventable blindness and promoting eye health around the world. Through her tireless advocacy and support, she continues to make a meaningful difference in the lives of individuals and communities in need.

Lorraine Smith's dedication to charitable causes serves as an inspiration to us all, reminding us of the profound impact that one person can have when they use their voice, their resources, and their platform for the greater good. As she continues to advocate for those in need and work tirelessly to create positive change, her legacy of compassion and generosity will endure for generations to come.

Lorraine Smith's remarkable contributions extend beyond her professional accomplishments, as evidenced by the numerous awards and honors she has received for her philanthropy, advocacy, and dedication to various causes.

In April 1991, Lorraine was recognized with the TRIC Diamond Jubilee Award for New Talent of the Year, marking the beginning of a long and illustrious career in the spotlight. Her talent and charisma endeared her to audiences, setting her apart as a rising star in the world of television.

In 2004, Lorraine made history as the first female rector of the University of Dundee, a position she held with distinction until 2007. Her tenure was marked by a commitment to fostering inclusivity and promoting the welfare of students, earning her widespread admiration and respect within the university community.

For her unwavering dedication to charitable causes, Lorraine was awarded an honorary Doctor of Laws from the University of Dundee in June 2008. This prestigious honor served as a testament to her tireless efforts to make a positive impact on the lives of others, embodying the spirit of service and compassion that defines her character.

In recognition of her outstanding contributions to charity and the armed forces, Lorraine was appointed Officer of the Order of the British Empire (OBE) in the 2012 New Year Honours. This prestigious accolade reflected her commitment to supporting those in need and advocating for causes close to her heart.

Lorraine's remarkable career in broadcasting and journalism was further honored in the 2020 Birthday Honours, where she was promoted to Commander of the Order of the British Empire (CBE). This prestigious title recognized her significant contributions to the field, as well as her continued dedication to charitable endeavors and philanthropic work.

Throughout her career, Lorraine has been a staunch supporter of the LGBT community, earning her the title of "one of Britain's cult gay icons" by Attitude magazine. In 2015, she was honored with the "Honourary Gay Award" at the Attitude Awards, recognizing her unwavering support and advocacy for LGBT rights.

In addition to her professional achievements, Lorraine has also been recognized for her service to the military, serving as an Honorary Colonel in the Black Watch battalion Army Cadet Force since June 2009. In November 2019, she was appointed National Honorary Colonel of the Army Cadet Force, further cementing her commitment to supporting the next generation of military leaders.

From her groundbreaking work in television to her tireless advocacy for charitable causes, Lorraine Smith's impact has been felt far and wide, earning her a place of honor and admiration in the hearts of many. Her accolades serve as a testament to her unwavering dedication to making the world a better place for all.

Lorraine Smith's involvement in scholastic and honorary appointments reflects her commitment to education, service, and leadership.

From April 2004 to September 2007, Lorraine served as the Rector of the University of Dundee, a position of great responsibility and influence within the academic community. During her tenure, she worked tirelessly to represent the interests of students and promote the university's values of excellence and inclusivity.

In recognition of her significant contributions to charity and her dedication to service, Lorraine was awarded an honorary Doctor of Laws (LL.D) from the University of Dundee in June 2008. This prestigious honor served as a testament to her commitment to making a positive impact on the world and her unwavering advocacy for those in need.

In June 2018, Lorraine received another esteemed honor when she was awarded a Doctor of Arts (D.Arts) degree from Edinburgh Napier University. This recognition underscored her exceptional achievements in broadcasting, journalism, and philanthropy, highlighting her status as a role model and inspiration to others.

Lorraine's commitment to the military community is also evident in her honorary military appointments. Since June 2009, she has served as the Honorary Colonel of the Black Watch Battalion of the Army Cadet Force, demonstrating her support for the next generation of military leaders and her dedication to honoring the sacrifices of those who serve.

In November 2019, Lorraine's contributions to the military were further recognized when she was appointed National Honorary Colonel of the Army Cadet Force. In this role, she continues to uphold the values of leadership, integrity, and service, inspiring others to make a positive difference in their communities and beyond.

Through her scholastic and honorary appointments, Lorraine Smith has demonstrated a steadfast commitment to education, service, and leadership. Her dedication to making a positive impact on the world serves as an inspiration to all who have the privilege of knowing her.

Lorraine Smith's personal life is a testament to her strength, resilience, and commitment to family.

From 1993 to 2005, Lorraine and her husband, Steve Smith, made their home in Cookham Dean, Berkshire, nestled along the serene banks of the Thames. Their idyllic life was enriched by the arrival of their daughter, Rosie, in 1994, who brought boundless joy and laughter into their lives.

Despite their relocation to Bourne End, Buckinghamshire, in December 2017, Lorraine's heart remained firmly rooted in her hometown of Dundee. Fondly referred to as an 'adopted Dundonian,' she has always held a special place in her heart for the vibrant city where she spent her formative years. Even as she ventured into new territories, Dundee remained a source of comfort and nostalgia, a place she would forever call home.

Lorraine's journey to motherhood has been marked by both joy and sorrow. While the arrival of Rosie brought immeasurable happiness, the pain of a miscarriage in 2000 cast a shadow over their lives. Yet, through it all, Lorraine and Steve remained steadfast in their love and support for each other, finding solace in their shared bond and the precious moments they shared as a family.

Beyond her roles as wife and mother, Lorraine is a passionate advocate for causes close to her heart. As a fervent supporter of Dundee United Football Club since 1987, she has embraced her role as an honorary patron with pride, embodying the spirit of loyalty and dedication that defines the club's fanbase.

In 2018, Lorraine bravely opened up about her experiences with the menopause, sparking a much-needed conversation about a topic often shrouded in silence and stigma. By sharing her story, she empowered other women to speak openly about their own experiences, fostering a sense of solidarity and support within the community.

Through the ups and downs of life, Lorraine Smith's unwavering love for her family, her hometown, and her fans shines brightly, illuminating the path for others to follow. Her journey serves as a reminder of the power of resilience, courage, and the bonds that unite us all.

Lorraine Smith's television career is a testament to her versatility and enduring popularity as a presenter and personality. From her early days on "Good Morning Britain" to her current role as the host of "Lorraine," she has graced the screens of millions of viewers with her warmth, charm, and wit.

Throughout the years, Lorraine has been a familiar face on a wide range of programs, showcasing her talents as a presenter, narrator, and even as a guest contestant. Highlights of her filmography include:

"Good Morning Britain" (1984-1992): Lorraine's career began on this popular morning show, where she honed her skills as a presenter and became a beloved fixture in households across the UK.

"GMTV with Lorraine" (1993-2010): Lorraine's role expanded on GMTV, where she presented various programs and segments, solidifying her reputation as one of the nation's favorite morning show hosts.

"This Morning" (2003-2005, 2016): Lorraine has made multiple appearances on this iconic daytime show, stepping in as a presenter and lending her expertise to discussions on a wide range of topics.

"Lorraine" (2010—): Since 2010, Lorraine has hosted her own self-titled program, where she continues to entertain and inform viewers with celebrity interviews, lifestyle segments, and topical discussions.

"The Sun Military Awards" (2016—): Lorraine has been involved in honoring the bravery and sacrifice of military personnel through her hosting duties on this annual awards show.

"RuPaul's Drag Race UK" (2019-2021): Lorraine made memorable guest appearances on this popular reality competition, delighting fans with her enthusiasm and support for the contestants.

"The Masked Singer" (2024): Lorraine surprised audiences as a contestant on this hit singing competition, showcasing her hidden talent and adding a touch of intrigue to the show.

Lorraine Smith's guest appearances on various television shows have added sparkle and charm to the small screen over the years. From game shows to talk shows, her vivacious personality has made her a welcome addition to any lineup. Here are some notable guest appearances:

Cluedo (1992): Lorraine brought her wit and charm to this classic game show, adding a touch of intrigue to the mystery-solving antics.

Surprise Surprise (1993-1995): As a guest on this heartwarming show, Lorraine delighted audiences with her warmth and genuine kindness.

The Mrs. Merton Show (1995): Lorraine's appearance on this iconic talk show provided laughs and memorable moments for viewers.

Shooting Stars (1997): Lorraine showcased her comedic chops on this irreverent comedy panel show, proving she's not afraid to have a laugh.

Lily Savage's Blankety Blank (2001): Lorraine's quick wit and infectious laughter made her a perfect fit for this classic game show.

The Jonathan Ross Show (2014): Lorraine charmed audiences with her wit and charisma on this popular talk show, sharing anecdotes and insights from her life and career.

The Cube (with daughter Rosie) (2021): Lorraine teamed up with her daughter Rosie for a special episode of this thrilling game show, showcasing their bond and competitive spirit.

The One Show (2023), (2024): Lorraine made multiple appearances on this beloved talk show, sharing stories and engaging with the hosts and audience.

Mary Makes It Easy (2023): Lorraine lent her expertise to this cooking show, sharing tips and tricks for making delicious meals with ease.

Whether she's cracking jokes on a comedy panel show or sharing heartfelt stories on a talk show, Lorraine's guest appearances always leave a lasting impression. Her infectious energy and genuine warmth make her a beloved presence on any television program, bringing joy and laughter to audiences around the world.

Film

Year	Title	Role
2014	Pudsey: The Movie	Cat (voice)
2023	Dfi Dudu and the Countdown	Narrator (voice)

Bibliography

- Lorraine Kelly's Nutrition Made Easy (Virgin Books, due January 2009)
- Lorraine Kelly's Junk-Free Children's Eating Plan (Virgin Books, 2007)
- Lorraine Kelly's Baby and Toddler Eating Plan (Virgin Books, 2002/2004/2006)
- Lorraine Kelly's Scotland (released 13 March 2014)
- The Island Swimmer (released 15 February 2024)[93]

Printed in Great Britain
by Amazon